Original title:
In the Island's Shadow

Copyright © 2025 Creative Arts Management OÜ
All rights reserved.

Author: Kieran Blackwood
ISBN HARDBACK: 978-1-80581-689-8
ISBN PAPERBACK: 978-1-80581-216-6
ISBN EBOOK: 978-1-80581-689-8

Whispers of the Forgotten Cove

There's a crab that dances quite absurd,
Its moves defy the wisdom of a bird.
It twirls and jigs, a true seaside star,
While fish all watch, saying, "Look at bizarre!"

Shells gossip tales of the day's lost hat,
While seagulls squawk, quite unsure where it's at.
A jellyfish floats, with a grace so meek,
While the sunbeams wink at the waves that peek.

Beneath the Canopy of Quiet Dreams

The parrot's jokes are a colorful fright,
Telling fish tales in the soft moonlight.
A monkey swings, dodging the coconut falls,
Teasing the crabs as they dance on the walls.

The stars look down, bright pinpricks of cheer,
As a shy little turtle approaches near.
He hiccups in rhythm, a splash on the ground,
And giggles arise from the leaves all around.

Secrets Held by the Tides

A sandcastle built with a laugh and a dare,
Stood firm till a wave came to give it a scare.
The shells on the beach hold secrets galore,
While a starfish chuckles on the damp, sandy floor.

The seashells gather for a gossip-filled chat,
"This tide really thinks it's the ruler of that!"
But waves only giggle, as they roll and cling,
While crabs don their hats—it's a whimsical fling!

Echoes of the Distant Shore

Old boats sit quietly, tales in their wood,
Whispers of fish caught where the currents once stood.
A seagull named Fred plays a trick on the breeze,
While a walrus waits, munching kelp with great ease.

The lighthouse beams shine like toothy grins,
As barnacles gossip about neighbors' sins.
They chuckle and sway, mixed with salt and with spray,
As laughter echoes throughout the bay.

The Lure of Sunlit Waters

A crab wore shades, quite proud and bright,
He danced with waves from morning till night.
Seagulls squawked jokes, as they flew by,
Witty remarks made the fishermen sigh.

Beach balls bounced with cheerful glee,
While sunscreen battles raged, oh me!
With slippery slides, friends laughed in the sun,
A day full of chaos, oh what fun!

Veiled by Ocean's Embrace

The tide rolled in with mischief afoot,
A sea turtle scoffed at a stuck flip-flop root.
Octopus chefs whipped up seaweed stew,
While dolphins played cards, with winnings due.

A fish slipped by in a silly disguise,
Complaining of fins, and sore scaly thighs.
Between the waves, laughter erupted,
Echoing tales of plans that erupted.

Tales from the Hidden Bay

Invisible pirates searched for their loot,
Only found a rubber duck, oh shoot!
They claimed it was treasure from times of yore,
But it squeaked too loud; they wanted no more.

Sunbathers snored, under floppy hats,
Dreaming of naps, and beach volleyball spats.
The sandcastle king built a magnificent throne,
Only to be toppled by wind's cheerful groan.

Reflections in the Silent Lagoon

In a quiet cove, a parrot squawked loud,
Mimicking laughter from an unseen crowd.
He practiced his lines for a comedy show,
While crabs debated on which way to go.

A seal balanced fish on his nose with flair,
Claiming it's just art, a fishy affair.
With every splash, giggles rang clear,
In the lagoon's heart, there was nothing to fear.

The Quiet Heart of a Sandy Cove

Seagulls gossip with the breeze,
A crab dons shoes, yet trips with ease.
The tide rolls in, then out again,
Whispering tales of fish and pain.

Lying low, a turtle grins,
Pirate dreams where laughter spins.
Shells gather secrets, pearls of jest,
Tickling toes as waves invest.

Sun-soaked laughter, silly songs,
Gathering where the goofball belongs.
Coconuts laugh as they sway,
A beach party in full display.

Friends all gather, no one cares,
In sandy seats, we swap our chairs.
The heart whirls in playful glee,
A day like this, just you and me.

Shadows of the Sunken Reef

Fishes dance in coral gowns,
While a lone shark wears swim shorts frowns.
Bubble parties in wild blue,
Giggling clams offer snacks, it's true.

A starfish strikes a pose so grand,
While octopus plays maracas with its hand.
Mermen sing with voices so high,
But they just can't seem to fly.

The reef's a scene of joy and fun,
Where every critter has a pun.
Sea cucumbers roll in glee,
For they know life's a big spree.

Underwater, laughter waits,
A dolphin teaches, "Dance, don't gait!"
In the deep, no room for strife,
Just silly games and underwater life.

Beneath the Mango's Gaze

Mango trees hold secret schemes,
Squirrels plot while dreaming dreams.
A lizard slips, nearly falls,
As laughter echoes through the halls.

Swinging low, the branches sway,
Frisky monkeys steal the day.
They chatter stories, play it cool,
While ants march on, their own parade rule.

Beneath the shade, we eat and cheer,
Tropical treats that disappear.
Juices splash as giggles rise,
The fruit is worth the sunny skies.

Picnic blankets, sprawled out wide,
As flavors burst, we cast aside.
Mango joy, so sweet, divine,
Beneath this tree, all hearts align.

Kisses of the Ocean Breeze

The ocean whispers soft and sly,
Tickles your ear, a breezy hi.
Shells sing songs of days gone past,
While waves concoct a party blast.

Breezes flirt with sunlit sails,
Pigeon pairs tell goofy tales.
The surfboard dances, twists and spins,
While laughter bubbles from within.

Flip-flops fly, a game of chance,
As seagulls join the crazy dance.
In salty air, the giggles blend,
A day of fun that knows no end.

With every wave, a secret shared,
The ocean's kisses, wild and bared.
In playful spirits, we engage,
Writing our stories on the page.

Shifting Shadows of the Bay

A seagull dropped a sandwich roll,
I laughed so hard, it took a toll.
The fish below just wiggled fake,
'We're not part of this silly mistake!'

The lighthouse blinked with quirky light,
A cat named Whiskers took to flight.
He danced along the rocky pier,
And all the fish just cheered, 'Oh dear!'

The boats all bobbed in funny rows,
While jellyfish wiggled to and fro.
They wobbled past in joyous glee,
'Join us, humans, you'll see our spree!'

The Ether of Distant Shores

A crab once claimed he owned a hat,
He posed for selfies, imagine that!
The waves just chuckled, 'Look at him go!'
As if the tide would steal the show.

A pirate parrot squawked a tune,
While dolphins danced beneath the moon.
They tried to outsing the silly gull,
But all fell quiet when the whale gave a grunt-full.

A treasure map was drawn in sand,
With X's marked by a little hand.
Not with gold, but pizza pie,
And all the locals ate and sighed.

Perpetual Twilight at the Water's Edge

A starfish peered out, eyes aglow,
'This beach is perfect, don't you know?'
He tried to surf, just fell instead,
While crabs all giggled, 'Off to bed!'

The tide rolled in with frothy cheer,
As squishy jelly danced near here.
'Can we get up?' the clams all cried,
'We'll make a splash, let's take a ride!'

A fish in specs read from a book,
He told tall tales with a crooked look.
And all the seashells clapped with glee,
'Next time, read to us under the sea!'

Lament of the Distant Sea

'I lost my sock!' a turtle sighed,
The octopus shrugged, 'Let's take a ride!'
They searched each wave, a quest so grand,
With hints from a crab, and guidance from sand.

An angry clam began to shout,
'Why wear one sock? It's such a drought!'
But as they danced, the tide came in,
And laughter bubbled; they forgot their sin.

At sunset's glow, they found the prize,
A sock adorned with sparkly ties.
They put it on the wigging fish,
And made a wish: 'May all have bliss!'

Beneath the Shadow of the Lanterns

As lanterns swing and sway,
We dance our cares away.
The fish look on, bemused,
We've got them all confused.

The coconut drinks fly high,
With laughter, we comply.
A parrot shades our chat,
Sipping tea while looking fat.

We stumble on the sand,
With buckets in our hand.
The crabs, they scuttle quick,
Avoiding our silly trick.

Beneath the bright moon's eye,
We laugh at the night's lie.
With dreams, we weave our schemes,
Creating joy in beams.

A Sojourn in the Sun's Caress

The sun smiles wide and bright,
As we bask in delight.
Forgotten hats may fly,
Chasing clouds as they sigh.

The seagulls squawk a tune,
Unaware of our swoon.
We dig a giant hole,
While our snacks play the role.

Ice cream drips down our chin,
A battle we won't win.
Sandcastles stand so tall,
While waves think they're the wall.

We take a silly plunge,
In water, we will lunge.
With shouts and splashes near,
A day full of good cheer!

The Ocean's Echo: A Distant Call

The ocean's voice, it sings,
Of mermaids and their flings.
We grab our shells to hear,
What tales might appear here.

A crab with quite a snap,
Tries to steal our sun nap.
With giggles we retreat,
That crab's got clever feet!

The waves whisper and tease,
A challenge with the breeze.
We juggle seashell prizes,
The ocean laughs in sizes.

As sunset takes its bow,
We'll treasure this somehow.
With echoes in our minds,
We leave the fun behind.

A Harbinger of Serene Waters

A boat drifts on the blue,
With snacks for just a few.
The fish wink as they pass,
Like they know our hidden sass.

The sails are flapping free,
We chat so joyfully.
A seagull steals our lunch,
It laughs with every crunch.

As waves gently sway us,
We find new ways to fuss.
The captain waves with glee,
He's lost his hat you see!

As twilight starts to crawl,
We muster one last call.
With laughter in our sails,
We sail on silly trails.

Tempests of the Untold Past

A seagull squawks with all its might,
While pirates dance in moonlit night.
Their treasure's gone, just coins remain,
They don't recall which way they came.

A ship that sails on cups of tea,
With spoons for oars, oh, what a spree!
The captain claims he hides a map,
But really, it's just a funny nap!

They head for shores of jelly beans,
And fight with crabs for pirate beans.
The ghostly crew, they laugh and sing,
While chasing after candy bling!

The tales they weave, a tangled jest,
Of briny snacks and treasure chests.
Though tempests rise, they brave the storm,
With giggles that keep spirits warm.

Gales and Glimmers of Forgotten Tales

In pirate hats with feathers bright,
They sail the seas by morning light.
With fishy friends, they play charades,
While mermaids giggle in the glades.

A storm blows through, it starts to rain,
But wait—it's just a lemonade train!
They sip and slide, oh what a rush,
As waterspouts begin to blush.

Forgotten tales of olden days,
In snail-shell boats, they find new ways.
The captain trips on his own shoe,
And walking the plank seems so askew.

With sails that flap like drunken birds,
They sing of snacks, not ancient swords.
These gales can't keep their spirits low,
As laughter is the way to go!

Songs of the Siren's Rest

A siren sings with fishy grace,
Her voice is like a wild goose chase.
She lures the sailors, what a trick,
But they just giggle—oh, so slick!

In waters deep, where bubbles play,
They splash around in seaweed fray.
The songs morph into silly chants,
And even crabs join in their dance.

They trade their swords for rubber ducks,
And swordfish joust with silly luck.
With mermaid wigs and wigs gone wild,
They laugh just like a carefree child.

At sunset's glow, with jokes that last,
Forgotten gold seems not so fast.
For treasures lie in joy and jest,
In waters where they find their rest.

The Enchantment of Coastal Shadows

Beneath the palms, shadows grow tall,
Where chickens dream and seagulls squall.
They play a game of hide and seek,
And tell fish tales that spring a leak.

Sandcastles rise, but then they flop,
With crabs in charge, they're bound to stop.
The waves applaud with foamy cheer,
As laughter echoes bright and clear.

A turtle joins the hula dance,
While flip-flops fly in silly prance.
In coastal shadows, mischief brews,
With every step, they tread on shoes.

As dusk draws near, the jokes unfold,
With stories shared of brave and bold.
Each shadow hides a giggle spree,
An enchanted night, wild and free.

Serenade of the Hidden Lagoon

Bubbles rise and fish do dance,
A clam with dreams of romance.
Crabs in tuxedos, ready to sway,
Under the moonlight, they frolic and play.

Seashells gossip, whispering tales,
Of a dolphin who thinks he sails.
The starfish laugh and wave their arms,
While the octopus charms with colorful balms.

A turtle wears sunglasses, quite a sight,
While jellyfish twirl, glowing at night.
A coconut floats in the breeze so sweet,
Where fish wear hats, now that's a treat!

With each splash, the lagoon smiles wide,
Life's a party, come join the ride!
In the splashy scene, all worries are foes,
Here in the laughter where silliness flows.

Driftwood Memories and Salty Kisses

Driftwood sits with stories old,
Of seagulls dressed in jackets bold.
It dreams of ships that sailed the sea,
And every barnacle's history!

Salty air whispers jokes so fine,
As crabs skitter and tumble, divine.
A wave that trips but doesn't care,
Makes fish giggle in salty air.

With flip-flops lost and nets to mend,
The sun laughs down, it's a lazy trend.
Smiles grow wide on sunburned cheeks,
As sandcastles lean with legs at their peaks.

At dusk, the beach throws a wild ball,
Where shadows dance and no one's small.
Under the stars, just take a chance,
Join the driftwood for a final dance!

The Waiting Tide's Embrace

The tide rolls in, with a sassy grin,
Making jellyfish lose their spin.
Sandcastles wonder if they can stay,
While the waves chuckle and sweep them away.

Seagulls squawk with a comic flair,
Jousting over chips in the salty air.
An octopus falls for a whimsical tune,
Clapping along beneath the moon.

A crab and a clam share a cup of tea,
While starfish dip in a wild jubilee.
A dolphin wears a goofy hat,
As all the fish giggle, 'Imagine that!'

As the tide pulls back, they wave goodbye,
With shells that wink and catch the eye.
The waiting game is filled with mirth,
For sea creatures who savor their time on earth.

Beneath the Waves' Tender Caress

Beneath the waves where silliness sways,
A fish jokes about the humans' gaze.
A turtle chuckles at his own shell,
While sea cucumbers cast a spell.

Whales hum songs of a grand parade,
While crabs march off on an ocean crusade.
A clam with a grin opens wide,
Offering treasures from the tide.

Anemones dance in a vibrant swirl,
As clownfish bubble in a playful twirl.
The ocean floor's a vibrant stage,
Where every creature uncages their rage!

So if you dive where the sea stars glow,
Remember the laugh, the giggle, the flow.
For under the waves, in joyous flair,
Lies a world where laughter fills the air.

The Fragmented Light of Dusk

As the sun begins to snooze,
Seagulls play their evening blues.
A crab dances with fancy flair,
While coconuts roll without a care.

There's a fish who thinks he sings,
Making the waves wear tiny rings.
But his notes are more of a splat!
Even the dolphins go 'What was that?'

The shadows stretch like lazy cats,
Hiding treasures, and hats, so that,
A hermit crab hops in surprise,
Thinking it found a home that flies.

With laughter echoing through the night,
Under the stars, all feels just right.
Each shadow a friend, none brave nor shy,
As the moon winks and says, 'Oh my!'

Lullabies of the Ocean's Heart

The tides hum softly on the shore,
While starfish play their ancient lore.
A turtle snores, his dreams alight,
In seashells sung as pillows tight.

Wet seaweed wraps around his head,
He chuckles in his sleepy bed.
A crab in PJs, taking a nap,
Dreams he's the captain of a lap.

While jellyfish float in dance so grand,
Adrift in night, they take a stand.
They jive and glide, then trip and fall,
Making everyone laugh, that's all.

The moonly waves whisper fun tales,
Of fish on bicycles and dolphin sails.
As they sway beneath the starry art,
The ocean's lullabies mend every heart.

Crescendo of the Coastal Dawn

Morning peeks, stretching its paws,
Sunbeams tickle the salty jaws.
Seashells giggle under bright skies,
While each tide whispers sweet surprises.

Crabs and clams start their lovely dance,
Doing the cha-cha in ocean's trance.
A pelican flops with comedic grace,
As he gobbles up breakfast with a rush and chase.

The sun yawns wide, the colors twirl,
Fish parade with a shiny swirl.
A dolphin jokes, 'Look at my trick!'
And belly flops with each little flick.

Their laughter rings, a bright serenade,
As day breaks forth, in joy you'll wade.
Every wave a note in the song,
In coastal dances where we belong.

The Secret Life of Umbrella Trees

Clad in green with a sun-kissed coat,
Those trees hide tales, oh what a note!
They whisper secrets in the breeze,
'This squirrel thinks he's quite the tease!'

A chameleon with style so neat,
Swaps his shades with such a beat.
Turns into green, then blue with flair,
Covering up from the curious stare.

Their shadows beckon to birds and bees,
Who giggle at their swaying knees.
A sloth hangs low with a lazy yawn,
Blending with leaves till the break of dawn.

But underneath their leafy cloak,
Is a party where the critters joke.
As wind chimes jingle with joy and cheer,
Those umbrella trees, we hold so dear.

Journey to the Forgotten Tidepool

The tidepool waits with open arms,
Where hermit crabs prance, flaunting charms.
Seaweed dancing, a slippery stage,
While clams play chess, like wise old sage.

A starfish slipped on a patch of ooze,
Giggling softly, sharing the blues.
"Oh, what a splash!" the little fish said,
As seagulls chuckled, crows in their bed.

We found a lost boot, a treasure indeed,
A home for a crab, on that we agreed.
With a wave and a wink, the tides rolled in,
As laughter echoed, the day to begin.

The sea foam swirls with funny tales,
Sailors tell stories as laughter sails.
In puddles of joy, the world seems bright,
In our tidepool home, what a wacky sight!

Memoirs of an Abandoned Shore

On a quaint beach where lost things rest,
A flip-flop winks, feeling quite blessed.
Seagulls gossip with shells, dismayed,
About the crabs that made their parade.

A bottle dreams of a message inside,
While driftwood wonders when it will ride.
A jellyfish moonwalks, showing its flair,
In the salty air, the laughter we share.

The sandcastles crumble, their reign expired,
While tourists lament, their dreams all retired.
But the tide rolls on, with a giggle and gleam,
Carving out stories like a whimsical dream.

Waves clap their hands at the folly so grand,
As barnacles chuckle, stuck firm on the sand.
In this merry chaos, we all sing along,
At the beach of lost things, we all belong!

Eldritch Currents and Echoing Moons

By the eerie sea where shadows play,
The crabs debate the rules of ballet.
"Two left feet!" they snicker, while fish laugh it up,
As starry-eyed jelly, floats by like a pup.

The octopus juggles with rocks and seaweed,
While the dolphins crack jokes, at their own misdeed.
"Remember the time we caught a surprise?
A surfboard instead of a line or two spies?"

Tides whisper softly, in riddles and rhymes,
As shells hold secrets of magical times.
Echoing moons smack the waves with a cheer,
While the old lighthouse chuckles, "I'm still here!"

With swirling currents directing the plot,
And creatures who giggle at mischief and rot.
In this ocean dance, hilarity flows,
Be it tales of the deep, or raucous sea shows!

The Language of Forgotten Sands

Once upon dunes where the giggles roam,
Sandcastles chatter, claiming their home.
A grain tells tales of a wave's wild fall,
While beach balls bounce, in a free-for-all.

The sun plays peekaboo, hiding away,
As flip-flops trot on, ready to sway.
"Hey, look at me!" a lost kite proclaims,
But the wind just sighs, "You'll never change names."

The sea whispers jokes to the driftwood trees,
While sea turtles ponder the flavors of breeze.
"Let's race the tide!" a starfish suggests,
While clowns of the ocean try on new vests.

So dance with the grains, as laughter abounds,
With whispers of jest in the shuffling sounds.
Life's a big playground where fun never ends,
Forever we play, in the sands with our friends!

Where the Mangroves Whisper

Beneath the boughs, a crab does dance,
A wiggly jig with no chance of romance.
Fish wear their scales like shiny ties,
While the pelicans ponder their fishy lies.

A starfish strikes a pose, so grand,
Claiming sea floor as his stand.
Oysters gossip, pearls in tow,
As the clownfish giggles, 'Look at my glow!'

The sun takes a dip, oh what a splash,
While sea snails race in a hasty dash.
A conch shell cheers for the wavy crew,
While a heron wonders, 'What's my next view?'

With laughter echoing through leafy limbs,
Nature sings loud, nimbly on whims.
They play in the shade, the mangroves' sway,
Where silliness reigns—it's just another day!

The Veil of the Evening Tide

As moonbeams tiptoe on the sea,
Crabby critters shout, 'It's time for tea!'
Starfish hold a soirée, bright and bold,
Telling tales of treasures yet untold.

The laughter of waves, a bubbly sound,
Shells do the limbo, all around.
Seagulls squawk jokes, much to the delight,
Creating a ruckus on this starry night.

Jellyfish glow like disco balls,
Inviting all to dance and sprawl.
With a flick and a flop, they waltz away,
Giggling softly, they'll sway and play.

The tide pulls tight, with a comical wink,
As seaweed tangles, the fishy folk link.
Under the stars, they frolic in pride,
In a world where folly takes a ride!

Dreams Crafted in Sand

In the golden grains, a fortress stands,
Built by the hopes of tiny hands.
With buckets and spades, the kids do play,
Creating castles that might wash away.

A crab in a hard hat inspects the walls,
Deep in thought, as the seagull calls.
Beach balls bounce like playful suns,
While seagulls squawk, scoring funny runs.

The tide rolls in, the sandcastles sigh,
As water creeps close, oh how they die!
Yet laughter erupts, no tears allowed,
'Let's build again!' they cheer, oh so proud.

With every wave, a new start begins,
As the sun sets low, casting golden sins.
Joy mingles with salt, as day meets its end,
With dreams crafted in sand, we shall mend!

Echoes on a Wistful Breeze

A leaf on the wind takes flight with glee,
Painting the air, 'Look at me, whee!'
Dancing and twirling, it calls out loud,
To the gulls overhead, both silly and proud.

The breeze brings whispers of mischief near,
As crabs in tuxedos start a cheer.
Jellybeans tumble, oh what a scene,
As sand dollars join in, all dressed in green.

With each playful gust, a story unfolds,
Fishes remark about weather so bold.
The sky wears a smile, the stars align,
To share in the joy of this evening divine.

So laugh with the tide, let your worries cease,
Among winds and waves, find your piece.
With every echo and riddle that teases,
The shore tells tales that bring such eases!

Nightfall over Coral Dreams

As the sun dips low, the fish start to dance,
A crab in a top hat, seeking romance.
The starfish wear shades, looking quite sly,
While turtles in tuxedos glide blissfully by.

The seaweed's a party, all wriggly and bright,
An octopus juggles, a comical sight.
Seahorses tango, with flair and with zest,
Meanwhile, the dolphunkers just take a rest.

The moon's a disco ball, all sparkly and round,
While jellyfish float, making beats out loud.
The tide brings the laughter, it bubbles and brews,
As the shells keep the rhythm with their clinky-clank blues.

So if you should wander when night starts to fall,
Join the festivity, the grand aquatic ball.
With giggles and splashes, it's pure underwater,
In this watery realm, there's no need for a martyr.

Tales from the Tidal Zone

Once a clam had a dream, to dance on the sand,
But his shell was too heavy, and he didn't quite stand.
A fish whispered softly, 'Just wiggle your tail,'
And the clam laughed so hard, he popped out of the pale.

There's a hermit who borrowed a crab's fancy shell,
Now he struts with pride, it fits him quite well.
The tide rolls in, bringing stories anew,
Of pirates and mermaids, oh, if only they knew!

The seagulls are cackling, their jokes make us groan,
As they feast on the treats that float in from the lone
Caterpillar turtle, who thinks he's a frog,
Yet swims with such grace, like a true little hog.

So gather around for this wild tale we weave,
In the realm of the waves, where nobody grieves.
With laughter and shrieks, oh, the fun will commence,
In this tidal zone, where silliness makes sense!

Whispers of the Crescent Moon

At the peak of the night, the moon starts to grin,
A pufferfish chuckles, 'Let the mischief begin!'
Clams are in sneakers, running a race,
As dolphins do flips, putting smiles on each face.

Crabs gather round for a game of charades,
Where they mimic the whales and their grand escapades.
The clumsy old shrimp trips over a shell,
And the crowd erupts in laughter, oh, what a swell!

A glow-in-the-dark jelly performs with finesse,
Twinkling like stars, in their neon dress.
The soft coral giggles as it sways to the beat,
While the sea cucumbers tap dance, oh, so sweet.

So let the crescent light guide our merry parade,
As the ocean's own players put on their charade.
With whispers of joy carried over the tide,
In this moonlit revelry, we take so much pride.

Harmonies of the Evening Tide

When the day turns to dusk, the waves start to hum,
A chorus of critters, oh, here they all come!
The flounders are flapping, the seahorses sway,
In the harmony fest where everyone plays.

A lobster on drums keeps rhythm with flair,
While snails on guitars strum tunes in the air.
The fireworks fizz from the clams' playful pop,
As the starfish takes center, their dancing won't stop!

With every soft swell, the night witnesses cheer,
As the plankton glow bright, twinkling near.
The sea turtles cluck like real grumpy old men,
Teaching fish to waltz, time and time again.

So join in this revel, let laughter abound,
In the evening's embrace, where joy can be found.
With the harmonies rising and the echoes at play,
We'll dance 'til tomorrow, in a splashing ballet!

Reflections Through Gnarled Roots

Gnarled roots twist and tangle wide,
Roots like fingers, where secrets hide.
A crab scuttles, doing the cha-cha,
Dancing boldly without a 'ha-ha'.

The pond's a mirror of sleepy fish,
Who throw glances at a soggy dish.
Nearby, a bird with a splashy quirk,
Sings off-key, but still, it works!

A frog leaps high, a glitch in the pond,
As turtles snicker, of this they're fond.
With every bop, there's laughter in air,
Nature's jesters—so wild, so rare.

Under flaming skies, the roots all yawn,
As night descends, and the stars are drawn.
Here, every giggle, every cheer,
Is nature's laughter, loud and clear!

The Last Light of a Wandering Breeze

The breeze tiptoes through the tall grass,
Carrying whispers of a blundering mass.
A wise old parrot tells a joke,
While waves giggle, with a bubbly poke.

The sun hangs low, like a dingy sponge,
Casting shadows where the crabs plunge.
A flip-flop sailing through the air,
Bounces off a fish with elegant flair!

With each gust, new tales unfold,
Of a sassy seagull in a cloak of gold.
He struts on the shore, like he's a star,
While clams roll their eyes at the ridiculous par!

As twilight winks and the skies turn red,
The laughter of day forges ahead.
A breeze that's silly, a playful tease,
Rolling soft jokes through tropical trees.

Whispers Beneath the Palm Trees

Palm trees gossip, swaying in crew,
With coconut tops full of morning dew.
A squirrel dashes with a nut in tow,
Is it snack time or a squirrel show?

Underneath, the sand giggles light,
At every tumble of children's delight.
A hermit crab dons a shoe that's found,
And struts, struts, struts all over the ground.

Whispers float like bubbles of air,
As a clam contemplates life without a care.
He sighs at the weight of his shell's design,
While laughing out loud—what a life divine!

As night creeps in, stars twinkle bright,
Lending their laughter to the whimsical night.
Under palm fronds, stories collide,
In the gentle cadence of this wild ride.

Echoes of a Forgotten Shore

On the beach where the sea meets the land,
There's a beach ball caught in a tireless stand.
It wobbles and rolls as if it can speak,
As seagulls cackle, quite sly and cheek.

Footprints of quirky visitors roam,
Each telling tales of this sandy home.
A starfish grins with his five-pointed charm,
While jellyfish bounce, oh so alarmed!

A sandcastle squats with grandeur proud,
Till a wave comes crashing, laughing loud.
The towers topple as the tides roar,
Nature's way of making everyone sore!

Fleeting glances of shells, bits of lore,
Echo softly on this humble shore.
With each passing tide, laughter and play,
Unfolding the stories of yesterday!

Beneath the Crescent Waves

Seagulls squawk with silly grace,
While crabs do a quirky race.
The fish wink as they swim past,
Playing games and having a blast.

An octopus wearing a hat,
Hides out under a big old mat.
Jellyfish twirl with a jelly jig,
All while chasing a dancing twig.

Shells whisper secrets, soft and sweet,
As shells join in for a tiny beat.
Turtles trip in a wobbly line,
Chasing after the shimmery brine.

Laughter bubbles up from the spray,
As waves dance merrily away.
In this silly ocean delight,
Everything seems just right tonight.

Silhouettes at Dusk's Embrace

One-legged flamingos paint the sky,
As dolphins leap and flutter by.
Penguins have their evening waddle,
While turtles giggle in a muddle.

Lobsters throw a beachy ball,
While starfish practice their grand crawl.
In the glow, they dance and prance,
Making quite the funny stance.

Coconuts fall with a playful thud,
And critters gather for the flood.
Underneath the blinking stars,
Everyone's joking from near and far.

So, take a seat upon the shore,
Join this mirth, we could use more.
When silhouettes come out to play,
The ocean surely laughs away.

Echoing Lullabies of the Deep

A whale sings tunes that tickle ears,
As clownfish giggle, banishing fears.
The seaweed sways, a long green arm,
Holding close each fish's charm.

Starfish serenade with cheeky flair,
While crabs tap-tap without a care.
Anemones sway in rhythm and rhyme,
These silly songs are simply sublime.

Dolphins join with playful flips,
And sea turtles make their funny quips.
Lullabies echo through the blue,
Filling the sea with joyful hue.

As bubbles rise from the ocean floor,
Each creature whispers, "There's so much more!"
In the depths where shadows roam,
They find mischief, laughter, and home.

The Dance of Driftwood Dreams

Driftwood waltzes upon the tide,
With barnacles as its joyful guide.
They twirl and swirl in the salty air,
A crusty ball where no one's bare.

Seashells clap with a gentle cheer,
While sea otters glide, bringing the beer.
Every wave brings a new surprise,
As they giggle under the bright blue skies.

With each splash, the laughter flows,
From sandy toes to seaweed bows.
Even the tides can't hold back glee,
As the ocean dances, wild and free.

So join the driftwood, merge your dreams,
In this playful world where laughter gleams.
With every laugh, the sea will beam,
Follow the whims of those driftwood dreams.

Reflections of a Starlit Horizon

The moon's a giant disco ball,
While crabs dance like they'd never fall.
A fish complains about the tides,
Waves are just a fishy ride.

Bamboo trees sway, their secrets spill,
Parrots squawk, 'It's quite a thrill!'
Turtles cruise on sandy roads,
While seahorses share their codes.

Stars are just the sun's bad hair,
They twinkle with a cosmic flair.
Jellyfish float, quite unaware,
That their tentacles cause despair.

So gather 'round, let's share a laugh,
While coconut crabs teach the math.
Life's a jest beneath this glow,
On a starlit path, let's take it slow.

The Song of the Distant Horizon

The sun sings loud, a sunny song,
While flamingos dance all day long.
Fish in sunglasses swim with style,
Making waves with each silly smile.

Octopus plays the ukulele,
Singing tunes that are quite sprightly.
Seagulls laugh with a cheeky squawk,
While clams join in, they love to rock.

A beach ball rolls with a playful fumble,
While crabs throw sand, it's quite a jumble.
Waves clap hands like a crowd in cheer,
As the sunset draws the night near.

So let's join the merry spree,
With laughter echoing in the sea.
Together we'll find where joy aligns,
In this quirky world, where fun shines.

Visions of Lost Horizons

The horizon yawns, a sleepy sight,
While turtles dream through the warm night.
Lobsters plot their escape plan,
From dinner tables where they ran.

Parrots gossip, much to explore,
About the fish from the ocean floor.
Anemones wave with festive cheer,
As the end of the day draws near.

Mermaids giggle, causing a splash,
While dolphins play in a fancy dash.
A seaweed party awaits, oh dear,
It's a shindig that you can't miss here.

So embrace the mischief, take a chance,
Join the critters in their ocean dance.
Life is wacky beneath the skies,
Where even the waves wear funny ties.

Beneath the Palms

Palms sway like dancers in a trance,
As crabs rehearse their sideways dance.
Coconuts fall with a thud and boom,
While toucans plan a dinner room.

The breeze tells jokes, oh what a tease,
While sea urchins make a scene with ease.
Clams share tales of the day gone by,
And even fish give a wink and sigh.

A sandcastle leans, just a bit too tall,
While shells snicker, "Watch it fall!"
The starfish cheer for a new design,
Hoping their art will truly shine.

So bring your laughter, come join the fun,
Under the palms, where we've just begun.
Together we'll frolic in the sun's warm rays,
Crafting memories for our wacky days.

Stories Lie

Once a sea snail dreamed of flight,
Claimed it soared away from sight.
A fish agreed, "I've seen it race,
Through clouds and stars, such a pace!"

A clam once boasted of a treasure,
In a chest of untold pleasure.
Turns out it held only sand and glee,
But who cares? It sings merrily!

Jellyfish spin tales of night cruising,
While dolphins disrupt with joyous boozing.
Their wild tales tumble, what a bunch,
You can't help but giggle at their punch.

So gather close, let stories thrive,
In this silly place where dreams arrive.
With laughter echoing through the tide,
These whimsical tales are our greatest pride.

Drifting Dreams on Salty Waves

A seagull stole my sandwich today,
It flapped its wings and flew away.
I chased it down the sandy shore,
Screaming loud, 'Come back for more!'

The crab danced sideways, pinching my toe,
I laughed so hard, could hardly show.
Shells giggled as the waves rolled in,
Whispering stories of my win.

Floating on a bright blue float,
My sunscreen's melting, what a note!
The sun could fry an egg, they say,
But all I want is to laugh and play.

As dolphins leap, I join their cheer,
Who knew the ocean held such beer?
In salty dreams, our worries fade,
A world of giggles is lovingly made.

Heartbeats Between the Tides

My flip-flop's missing, where could it be?
A pelican's nesting, just wait and see.
With a wink, it swipes my spare shoe trick,
Suddenly, my walk feels quite slick!

Sandcastles formed and then they fall,
A wave rolls in, oh what a brawl!
The other kids start pointing and laugh,
But I'm the king! I'll take my half!

Pineapple juice falls down my chin,
Sticky fingers, I'm making a win.
A sunburned nose adds to my flair,
Who needs a mirror? I don't really care!

The tide pulls back with a playful grin,
Inviting my heart to jump right in.
With every splash, a joy will arise,
In the dance of waves, I find my prize.

The Dance of Morning Mist

The morning mist begins to sway,
As if it's dancing, come what may.
Jellyfish wearing top hats, quite grand,
Playing tag with gulls on the sand.

Seaweed waltzes with great delight,
While starfish skip by, oh what a sight!
Laughter bubbles in the salty breeze,
As crabs do the cha-cha with such ease.

Seagulls join in, flapping their wings,
Convinced they are the queens of springs.
A crab in a tux, they poke and tease,
While the ocean hums a tune with ease.

But as the sun starts to rise and peak,
The dance slows down, the waves grow sleek.
The mist retreats, the fun's on hold,
But what a sight, a tale retold!

Tales Told by the Sea's Embrace

Gather 'round for tales so bright,
Whispers carried on waves at night.
A dolphin who drank too much salt,
Declared it was time to waltz—what a jolt!

Seashells gossip under the moon,
About fish that dream of being goons.
A crab that lost his favorite shoe,
And sang a song of the ocean blue.

An octopus painting a canvas wide,
In colors that made even seas sigh.
The jellyfish glows, what a splendid show,
While the clams cheer on in a row!

Their laughter echoes across the bay,
As seagulls swoop in to join the play.
The waves clap hands, with a foamy cheer,
While tales unfold, both far and near.

Navigating the Heart of Calm Waters

In calm waters, a sailor yawns,
While fish perform their early cons.
Crashing waves are taking a break,
While a sea turtle takes a cake.

Pirate ships sail with a puff of smoke,
But the captain's had quite enough joke.
Mermaids laugh, tossing seaweed flair,
As gulls steal their snacks without a care.

The compass points to the snack bar, friend,
While jellyfish join in, their lights they send.
A game of tag starts with slippery fun,
In the heart of calm, the race has begun!

But when the sun sets, the laughter dies,
As fishy dreams dance in their eyes.
The waters sleep, so peaceful, so pure,
And yet, tomorrow, more mischief for sure!

The Poetry of Ebb and Flow

The tide sings songs of ebb and flow,
While chips of wood dance in a row.
Seagulls squawk as they flutter about,
Their antics in air, leaving no doubt.

A wave comes laughing, tickles the sand,
Its giggles are heard across the land.
Starfish cheer, forming a conga line,
While an octopus declares, "This is fine!"

Shells play hide and seek as they sway,
While crabs wear top hats and shout, "Hooray!"
The ocean's an artist, splashing, it seems,
Creating laughter in sunlight beams.

At the end of the day, when shadows grow tall,
And all the sea creatures heed the call.
They whisper softly, "What a good show!"
As the poetry of tides continues to grow.

Dreams Adrift on Tidal Winds

Sandy toes and fishy dreams,
A crab in flip-flops, or so it seems.
Seagulls squawk with flying flair,
While sunburnt tourists lose their hair.

A dolphin's dance makes waves of cheer,
As dolphins whisper, "Let's make this clear!"
A beach umbrella sails away,
Chasing the sun, or playing the prey!

The seaweed tickles at our feet,
As children giggle, the day's a treat.
But watch that wave, it's sneaky and sly,
It laughs with a splash, oh me, oh my!

Surfboards wobble, laughter erupts,
As jellyfish suit-wearers do jumps.
With tidal winds, our worries are tossed,
Floating on laughter, we count the cost.

Secrets Beneath the Coconut Canopy

Coconuts tumble, oh what a sight,
Each one holds secrets of the night.
Monkeys gossip in leafy retreats,
Trading tales of fruity feats.

A squirrel dressed in sunglasses bold,
Claims he's the king, or so I'm told.
Banana peels serve as slippery slides,
While hidden treasures the island hides.

Palm fronds wave with a sassy air,
Whispers float like the tropical flair.
A mango's secret, sweet and divine,
Is that it dreams of being a wine!

Under the leaves, the shenanigans brew,
As critters dance in a coconut crew.
The laughter echoes, tickling the ground,
In this fruity paradise, joy's all around.

Lighthouses of Forgotten Souls

Once bright beacons, now they snore,
Guiding ships to an ancient shore.
With beams of light that flicker and sway,
They tell of sailors who lost their way.

Old seagulls perch with tales of yore,
Each squawk a hint of sea folklore.
They share the gossip of mermaids' charms,
While pirates sing of their old alarms.

The lighthouse keeper's socks, mismatched,
A fashion choice that time dispatched.
His kettle whistles a tune off-key,
As shadows dance to the sea's old spree.

With lanterns dim, spirits play tricks,
As the moon chuckles with wave-like kicks.
In forgotten corners, laughter unspools,
Echoes of joy from those ancient souls.

Murmurs from the Sunlit Cove

Breezes whisper through the palm fronds,
Tickling the ears of beach bum blondes.
Whimsical waves play tag on the shore,
As they tease the sand, shouting, "Want more!"

Cheers build up in a gamesome shout,
As crabs are crowned, just look at them prout.
A clam competes in the poetry slam,
With verses so deep, he's quite the jam.

The sun chuckles as umbrellas dance,
While floaties giggle in a silly prance.
The coolers chuckle, filled with delight,
Every sip a cheer, shining bright.

In this cozy nook, joy loves to hide,
Where laughter sparkles like the ocean's tide.
Murmurs of fun from the cove we crave,
Where memories linger like a playful wave.

In the Wake of Paradise

Sunshine spills on sandy toes,
Seagulls steal my chips, who knows?
Umbrellas topple, drinks go splat,
Beach fun's just a game of cat.

Tanned folks scatter like sand flies,
The ice cream truck, oh how it cries!
With each lick, a drip on my shirt,
While kids dive in the sand—oh, dirt!

Flip-flops squeak, a dance of grace,
Someone's hat's now on a dolphin's face.
Laughter bounces on ocean air,
Who knew vacation came with this flair?

At sunset's glow, we raise our cups,
To sunsets, shells, and coconut slups.
When day is done, the stars take their bets,
I'll take the fun, forget the regrets.

The Lone Fisherman's Lament

His rod's outstretched, the bait a feast,
The catch of the day? Just a sea beast!
Fish are laughing, such a cruel tease,
He's just made friends with a swarm of bees.

Baiting hooks, he feels quite bold,
While talking to crabs, a sight to behold.
With every cast, a story unfolds,
But the biggest laughs are from the gulls, so old.

He sits on the dock, a king on his throne,
Sharing his lunch with a stray, alone.
The waves chuckle, the breeze gives a cheer,
As he sneaks a backflip—oh dear, oh dear!

In his dreams, he feasts on a whale,
But wakes up at dawn with a soggy tale.
The fish may be clever, but he's got a plan—
Next time he'll bring a much bigger can!

Twilight Dances on Coral Strings

The sun winks low, a tender tease,
Twilight twirls with the gentle breeze.
Shadows stretch like rubber bands,
As laughter bubbles above the sands.

Colorful fish wear shades of pink,
While crabs hold a conga line in sync.
Starfish pursue a graceful dance,
While the moon plants a sparkly glance.

Cocktails splash in a coconut shell,
Mermaids' giggles ring out, oh so swell.
In this reef, where dreams take flight,
Nature's beauty makes everything right.

As night descends, the stars align,
We toast to the waves, sweet and divine.
A dance with the tides, oh what a fling,
Laughing out loud at what night will bring!

Memories Embroidered in Seafoam

Each wave whispers tales to the shore,
Of clumsy pirates who lost their score.
With tangled nets and slippery boots,
They'd fish for tales, and not for loot!

Seagulls overhead flaunt their style,
Diving for snacks, they stay awhile.
A beach ball flies, it's caught in the breeze,
And hits a kid with style—oh jeez!

Sandy castles stand tall and proud,
While giggles echo through the crowd.
The tide comes in, a sneaky foe,
It swallows the castles, but still we glow.

By fireside chats in the evening's glow,
We share the mischiefs that only we know.
With every wave that crashes free,
Our memories stitch time's tapestry.

The Veil of Misty Horizons

The fog rolled in with a cheeky grin,
Like a cat that stole the sun's own rays.
We stumbled round, lost in the din,
While seagulls mocked our foggy maze.

I tripped on rocks, laughed on cue,
As friends rolled eyes with playful jeers.
The mist said, 'Hey, I'll hide from you!'
While we waved back between our fears.

The horizon winked with a shimmer bright,
But all we got was grey's embrace.
Yet every chuckle turned wrong to right,
In our silly dance, we found our place.

And thus we faced the mystery wide,
Like explorers with gut-busting cheer.
In a foggy land where joy could hide,
We discovered laughter was always near.

Heartbeats Beneath Starlit Skies

The stars above wore twinkling hats,
As crickets chirped their nightly song.
We pondered life, and spotted bats,
In a universe where we belong.

With sandwiches strewn like a picnic fight,
Ants marched in queues to steal our snacks.
We laughed aloud, a comical sight,
As we dodged those tiny food attack hacks.

A shooting star made a dash for the moon,
We cheered it on with goofy glee.
Wishes flew like balloons in June,
Wrapped in laughter, wild and free.

So here's to nights of wit and jest,
With heartbeats matching the starry glow.
Under the cosmos, we're truly blessed,
Finding joy in the comical flow.

Beneath the Basswood Canopy

Beneath the trees, we made our fort,
With leaves as shields from buzzing bees.
We plotted tales of silly court,
Where squirrels were guilty of tree misdeeds.

A raccoon waved, thinking he's king,
While we donned crowns of acorn hats.
Laughter rang as we took to swing,
While battling pirates, fierce house cats.

The basswood whispered its leafy lore,
As shadows danced in joyous spright.
We shouted loud, 'Adventure's galore!'
Eager to chase the fading light.

Each laugh echoed, a secret shared,
In the kingdom of giggles, we made a stand.
Childish wonder, no one was spared,
In this wooden world, bright and grand.

Where the Sea Meets Solitude

The waves came crashing, a comic splash,
While we built castles that washed away.
With buckets and shovels, it was a bash,
Our sandy dreams would not stay.

A seagull swooped with a cheeky flair,
Stealing chips while we tried to eat.
We laughed and chased without a care,
As it danced in circles, quite the feat!

The shorelines played a game of tag,
With tides retreating like playful ghosts.
We twirled and spun, not one soul lagged,
From salty winds to seagull boasts.

So let the sea bring giggles loud,
As footprints fade on the golden sand.
In moments shared, we stand so proud,
In camaraderie, so sweet and grand.

Shores of Time Forgotten

Upon the sands, my flip-flops squeak,
While crabs laugh at my sunburned cheek.
Seagulls squawk a melody so bold,
As sunscreen tales and snacks unfold.

A treasure map with chips and dip,
Could lead to gold with a single slip.
I tripped on waves, they waved back too,
In laughter's arms, the ocean grew.

Mysterious shells whisper my name,
The fish all cheer, it's a shell game.
Barrels of giggles float like a kite,
In this funny realm, all feels so right.

So raise a toast with sand in your drink,
For time here dances on a pink wink.
Where shadows play tag with the breeze,
And life's a jest beneath the trees.

In the Embrace of Solitude

A craggy rock my throne so fine,
Where seagulls gossip, oh how they whine.
I sip my coconut, feeling so grand,
While waves do the cha-cha on the sand.

The sun sets fast on my solitary show,
As pine trees giggle, saying hello.
With no one to judge, I dance with a crab,
In this laughter's grip, the world is a fab.

Echoes of chuckles bounce off the shore,
Where solitude reigns, who could ask for more?
Footprints in sand, a whimsical spree,
Dance with the breeze, just you and me.

The tide rolls in with a bubbly cheer,
Whisking my woes, they disappear.
In quiet giggles, life finds its tune,
Under the watchful eye of the moon.

When Silence Speaks Volume

When the waves hush, and the world is still,
A crab in a tuxedo gives me a thrill.
Whispers of shells share secrets wide,
While fish in a junta take things in stride.

The palm trees sway with silent grace,
As squirrels play tag, a raucous race.
In this realm where laughter holds sway,
Silence chuckles, come out to play.

The breeze, a messenger, tickles my ear,
Saying wild things that I only half hear.
Oftentimes, the quiet's a peculiar friend,
With giggles hidden around the bend.

As shadows move, with a wink and a nudge,
Every moment here is a light-hearted judge.
For even in silence, joy finds its way,
An unspoken jest at the break of day.

Tides of Solitary Reverie

The ocean's pull is a quirky muse,
As I ponder life with mismatched shoes.
Seashells chuckle as they tumble down,
In moments like this, I wear a crown.

The breeze gives me riddles that twirl and spin,
As dolphins burst forth with a splashy grin.
I pretend to swim as they frolic around,
With laughter mingling under waves unbound.

Sipping dreams from a coconut shell,
I find happiness, oh how swell!
Waves bow down in playful dance,
In my soliloquy, life's an odd romance.

Here in solitude, I giggle and muse,
In tides of reverie, I have nothing to lose.
The sun dips low with a wink so sly,
And I'm left grinning at the cobalt sky.

A Ballad by the Waters' Edge

A crab danced sideways, oh what a sight,
With a tiny top hat, it felt just right.
Seagulls squawk, thinking they're so slick,
But they're all dodging a slippery fish stick.

The tide pulls back, a game we find,
With sandcastles laughing, a bit unrefined.
A clam with a grin, it shows off its shell,
While a wave crashes down, saying, "Oh well!"

The sun sets low, clouds painted bright,
A fish jumps out, what a funny flight!
With each splash and giggle, the day bows out,
A party by the shore—what it's all about!

In the moon's soft glow, the stars yell, "Play!"
As the ocean hums us a breezy ballet.
Together we dance, as if to declare,
That laughter's the anthem in salty sea air.

Twilight's Palette on a Distant Bay

A dog on the beach wore a sunhat quite tall,
Chasing seagulls who'd laugh and then sprawl.
While the waves just chuckled, slapping the shore,
The sun slipped away, wanting a bit more.

The boats rocked gently, swaying with glee,
As fish formed a band, strumming under the sea.
"We're not just the catch," they joyfully sang,
While a lobster played drums and the conch shell rang.

The colors grew wild, splashes of flair,
With popsicles melting in the warm evening air.
A child made a wish on a cloud's fluffy form,
While the tide winked back, "In this, you'll stay warm."

As stars began twinkling, the night made its claim,
The bay told its secrets without any shame.
With chuckles and bubbles, what a crazy display,
Twilight danced on canvas, in a joyous array.

Songs of the Sunset Shore

The gulls gave a concert, off-key and loud,
While the sand dunes giggled, feeling quite proud.
A crab joined the choir, singing out rude,
In a voice like a trumpet, oh what a crude!

The lighthouse was winking, a beacon of fun,
Telling the waves, "Hey, you're second to none!"
With each crashing wave, a joke from the deep,
The otters all rolled, in laughter they'd leap.

As twilight approached, the sun started to pout,
With colors exploding, it danced all about.
"Why does the ocean seem so full of cheer?"
It whispered a secret, "It's the company here!"

When shadows grew long, and the crickets began,
The moon joined the fun, with a wink and a plan.
Together we sang, under night's sparkling lie,
With laughter and joy, far too silly to die.

The Solace of Stormy Waters

A storm brewed up, clouds heavy with jokes,
The wind told secrets, teasing the folks.
Raindrops played tag on umbrellas near,
As sailors all laughed, filled with good cheer.

In the eye of the storm, a dolphin did flip,
With a splash and a giggle, it danced on the trip.
While thunder grumbled, as if it could play,
The sea roared with laughter, come join the fray!

The waves spun like dancers in a dizzying whirl,
While pumpkins on boats took a tumble and twirl.
A fish in a bowtie winked at the sky,
Saying, "With all this fun, who wouldn't fly high?"

As rain turned to drizzles, and the storm took its leave,
The sea calmed down, but still wouldn't grieve.
For laughter and joy, even in tempest's song,
Is the solace we need, to carry us along.

Sails of the Forgotten Horizon

A sailor once lost his boot,
It floated away, thinking it cute.
The fish all laughed; they couldn't resist,
A finned chase was their grand little twist.

The compass spun like a topsy toy,
With every turn, he found new joy.
Instead of land, he spotted a whale,
Who waved hello with a friendly tail.

His parrot squawked with a sunny squint,
"The sun's your guide, don't let it hint!"
But the sun took a nap and slept too long,
Leaving the sailor in a dance of wrong.

So with sails so tattered and torn,
He laughed aloud, feeling reborn.
For in the quirks of the open seas,
There's comedy found in the wildest breeze.

A Canvas of Shifting Tides

Each wave paints a picture anew,
With shades of turquoise and bright sky blue.
The seaweed waltzes in gentle delight,
As crabs put on shows under the moonlight.

A jellyfish floats with a bob and sway,
Looking for a pirate who lost his way.
He gnaws on the treasure, a shiny old shoe,
Claiming it's gold, which he swears is true!

Sandcastles rise then flop at a glance,
As seagulls tango in a feathery dance.
The tide giggles loud, splashing with glee,
Tickling the toes of folks by the sea.

A painter arrives with a bucket and brush,
His strokes and splashes create quite the hush.
"Oh dear," he sighs, after a slip and a spin,
"My masterpiece now looks like a cat's little kin!"

The Twilight Thrill of a Gentle Gale

At twilight, the wind whispers low,
Telling secrets only sailors know.
The clouds gather 'round for a chat,
While the stars giggle at a cheeky cat.

A crab named Fred stretched out with flair,
Said, "Why walk when you can dance in the air?"
He twirled on the shore, grooving in style,
As the shoreline laughed and winked all the while.

The moon's a big cheese, so yellow and round,
It draws all the leaping fish from the ground.
With a splash and a flip, they join in the fun,
Trying to catch rays, till the day is done.

The wind, like a jester, tickles their fins,
With a giggle so loud, all the mischief begins.
In the breeze of the night, laughter takes flight,
Under the watchful eye of the twinkling twilight.

Breath of the Ocean's Memory

The ocean's breath carries tales so sweet,
Of sailors who danced with fish on their feet.
With tales of adventure and pranks on the way,
It giggles and ripples, all night and day.

A dolphin leaped high with a chuckle and spin,
"Catch me if you can!" was the game he'd begin.
As a clam with a grin tried to join in the fun,
He ended up stuck, what a slippery run!

The tide made a mess of sandcastles grand,
As children all cheered with shovels in hand.
They played hide and seek with crabs on the shore,
In the ocean's embrace, there's always much more.

With whispers of laughter, the waves softly roll,
Each swell a reminder, a light-hearted goal.
For in every splash, every giggle we see,
Is the heart of the ocean, forever carefree.

www.ingramcontent.com/pod-product-compliance
Lightning Source LLC
Chambersburg PA
CBHW072119070526
44585CB00016B/1497